7

EFFECTIVE STRATEGIES

FOR ACHIEVING

SUCCESS

ADEOLA BABATUNDE

Special thanks to my wife (Bola) and Children (David, Daniel and Debbie) who gave me the time and space to write.

To the authors and teachers I have learnt from, for their guidance and support along the way.

To my clients who allowed me to share what I have learnt through relating with them.

Printed in the United States of America

©Adeola Babatunde 2014

info@adeolababatunde.com

ISBN: 978-1-326-05591-2

Published by :Adeola Babatunde Media

TABLE OF CONTENTS

INTRODUCTION

Everything we do in life is a choice, and I think most of us realise that. But what most people don't seem to realise is that everything we don't do in life is also a choice. Every day we choose to do some things and to not do other things.

Sometimes choosing not to do something is the wisest choice. However, there is a huge difference between choosing not to do something and choosing to do nothing.

Most people would like to change their life in one way or another. How about you? Are there areas of your life that you would like to change?

What is stopping you?

Anytime you want to, you can change your life, but just wanting to change is not enough. You must make a choice to change. Doing nothing and wishing things would change is the course most people choose. Consequently, nothing ever changes.

The thought of having a different life, or a different quality of life, is very appealing to most people. It's easy to imagine being in better physical condition, having a more rewarding career, and enjoying more meaningful relationships. But pretending doesn't get the job done, does it? Obviously, more is required.

We have all created our present situation by the choices we made in the past. If we chose to do nothing, then our situation reflects that. Recognising that we live in a world of our own creation means that we are responsible. If we don't like our life the way it is, then we are the ones responsible for making changes. Does the thought of change make you feel uncomfortable?

One of the most common reasons why people are uncomfortable with change is because they haven't yet accepted full responsibility. For some reason, it seems to be a natural tendency to shrink away from responsibility.

This kind of mindset creates helplessness. It means that we are looking for change outside of ourselves. We may look to our mates to make us happy, or we may look to our careers to make us feel fulfilled. In a situation like this, if things don't turn out the way we want, we tend to blame our mates or our careers. No one else can make you happy, that is up to you.

No career or other person can bring you satisfaction if you are dissatisfied with yourself. What you need to do is to liberate yourself.

Accepting responsibility is actually a very liberating experience. Once we recognise that we are the ones in control, it makes life much simpler. Granted, we can't always control what goes on around us, any more than we can control the weather. So what can we control?

We can control our response to everything that happens!

Understanding this concept is a vital key to improving the quality of your life.

Whatever happens, you are in complete control of your response. You decide what value any event has in your life. Once you make an evaluation, you have the freedom to choose what comes next.

If you're not happy with your physical condition, make a choice to change, starting today. Too much pondering and over analysing just allows the current situation to continue. Yes, we want to make wise choices. But we don't want to endlessly delay making a choice as we continue searching for the best solution. It all starts with a choice. If it seems overwhelming, pick one area of your life and start there. You don't need to dive into the deep end, but you do need to start taking action.

CHAPTER 1

DETERMINE WHAT YOU WANT IN LIFE

Do you know what your life purpose is? Are you searching for a clear, detailed idea about who you can and want to become?

Your life purpose is what you are meant to take with you from this life -- what you want to experience, understand or learn. Discovering it creates a lifetime filled with meaning, joy, clarity and centeredness.

Finding your life purpose starts with discovering what captivates your heart and runs like a thread through your life. A golden thread that weaves your destiny into a beautiful tapestry.

If you don't know your life purpose, a lot of life decisions are really guesses -- and guesses, like guessing on the multiple choice test of Life, can get you into trouble.

You are basically guessing at what would make you happy. And that makes as much sense as guessing from the yellow pages who you are going to let perform open heart surgery on you.

Important things should not be decided with a guess -- especially life defining and shaping choices that directly determine your level of happiness.

What is a Life Purpose?

A life purpose is a simple statement of the reason you exist, the purpose behind you living now on this planet. It is the reason you came into being and the way you will decide if your life was worth it.

While a life calling focuses on what you will do and become ... your life purpose speaks to what you will take from this life ... what you came here to experience, learn and understand.

Why Do I Need A Life Purpose?

It is easy to get lost in modern life, to lose your way. You can fall asleep at the wheel as your life gets consumed with the mundane details of life. Or, joy and meaning can start to evaporate when life starts to get hard.

Having a clear idea of your life purpose keeps you motivated, focused and able to tap into a pool of energy when you need to face challenges, because you understand the why behind the events in our life.

Once you know your purpose for living, it takes the guess work out of making important life decisions. When combined with your life calling, your area of mastery and your life path -- you can know what you are supposed to be doing with your life, instead of guessing. And that can save you a lot of money, headaches, heart aches and time.

If you do not know what you are supposed to do, then you are just guessing at what will suit you ... or you are settling for what you (or others, the media, culture or your generation define) think is best for you.

Guessing at who you are meant to become and what you are meant to do, is a lot like when you were learning the multiplication tables and you knew you should know the answer but didn't. You could guess, but you would never have bet your favourite toy or tonight's dessert on being right.

Well, going through life guessing .. is a lot like betting your career, your income, and your future happiness -- all on a not so good guess. And a guess, no matter how well educated -- is still a guess.

Do you know your life purpose?

If the answer is no, then isn't it about time to get serious and figure out what you are supposed to be doing?

Why haven't I found my purpose in life?

Sometimes we hold ourselves back from the very things we want to find most ... often because we fear how it will change us.

Finding answers to life's Biggest questions can be scary ... partly because once you find an answer, now you know what you want to do with your life ... and that can give you a whole new perspective on your life.

No More Excuses

If you have been hiding from life and feeling like you can skate by and not really try hard because you do not know what you are supposed to be doing ... you may feel uncomfortable with the responsibility of following through and going after what you want.

Mistakes become clear

Knowing your life purpose can reveal how well you have made choices in the past as well as challenge you to make better -- or different -- choices in the future. Like airing dirty laundry, your illusions of how smart your past choices were may become all too clear in the sunlight of understanding what you can here to learn and experience.

Changes to your current life

Some people worry that knowing their life purpose may mean you have to give up your current life and leave your family and friends. If you have the wrong job, are living in the wrong city, or hanging out with the wrong people ... you may feel very uncomfortable with having to say goodbye and move on.

Not all change is bad ... but most of it is uncomfortable. We cling to what we know and what feels safe.

Is it hard to find my purpose in life?

Given all this, it might seem like a hard thing to do, but it is not that hard to discover what your life purpose is. Why? Because your life purpose is hiding right beneath the surface of your life. Like a golden thread it snakes between the major events of your life and opens windows of opportunity.

So to find it, all you need to do is see your life with new eyes. To take a close look at the events, challenges and lessons of your life ... and see what life is teaching you ... or trying to.

How do I find my life purpose?

This simple four step plan helps you find your life purpose. It works by helping you explore a list of universal life themes and ingredients of mastery to discover your own, and them transform your personal life themes into a statement of your life purpose.

This process helps you begin to know yourself and can start a process which transforms your life.

- **Identify Your Life Themes**

Start by exploring what you care most about in life. To make it easy to get started, I have a list of 28 themes of life that represent the areas we come to learn about and experience.

Each of these life themes reflects a way of seeing the world. By reading a brief description of each, you can quickly find the ones that resonate with you or interest you.

Now you have a good starting point for defining your life purpose. If you cook, consider it grabbing some of your favourite ingredients of a dish to be named later.

- **Reflect on your life themes**

Next, you want to focus on the life themes that resonate most with you. It is time to see how they are already a part of your life in the movies you watch, the books you read and the conversations you have.

It is also nice to see where they are in your life -- your weekend hobbies, flipping through the channels during a few free moments or are they a major part of your career? It is also worthwhile to think about how they would be a part of your life if you had the time, money and resources you dream of.

- **Find "The Why" behind your themes**

Now, it is time to get look "behind the scenes and find the why behind why your themes".

What about these themes grab and hold your attention, get your riled up or make you happy? Finding the Why is a critical step most miss -- but it is where you start to hit pay dirt.

Why? Because this is what turns your world, tweaks your psyche, and reveals what makes these universal life themes unique and personal to you. It is not a step to miss.

- **Explore your mastery ingredients**

Once you know what your life themes are, it is time to explore the specifics of how you are to live out your life purpose. To do that, you want to explore and identify the ingredients of your area of mastery -- the things, people, places, activities, experiences, talents, problems and ideas you love to work with and think about.

Think of these are the tools in your toolkit that help you do everything you need to, to fulfil your life purpose -- and they make how you manifest your life purpose unique to you.

- **Create a life purpose statement**

You start by writing down your life themes and then adding in your mastery ingredients. Then start creating a statement that reflects what you want most, care most deeply about and want to leave this life having experienced, learned or understood.

What then is the fundamental step to achieving what you want in Life?. You must first find out your destination before you make the move.

You must develop your life plan which consists of your goals and your actual strategies of what you should do so that you will achieve your goals. Most people know what they want, but they never really have a clear plan on how they can achieve it. If you want to be successful, you must start from managing and planning for your future.

Some people talk about what they want but they never really put it into action and actually make their dream come true. This is the biggest difference between a successful person and a person who is struggling. Successful people are committed to their dreams and goals. They are willing to do whatever it takes to achieve that which they have set out to achieve in life.

While the circumstances of today don't determine what's possible your actions do. You may not be in control of the circumstances, but you are in complete control of the actions you take. That's where you actually have a choice. What you do with each day is really a response to your circumstances.

Each step you take in the direction of a goal or a dream will reveal new possibilities that you were unaware of before.

Many people will criticise the choices you make on the path to pursuing your dreams. Don't live your life according to other people's expectations.

They are not the ones who are going to live with the consequences of your actions.

What's more important to you? What people think about your situation today or that you ultimately end up where you want to end up?. The journey is often unglamorous, filled with days that will test your patience and build your character. The question you have to ask yourself is what you're willing to go through?

What are you willing to give up?

"Sacrifices must be made on the path" Ask yourself, what are you willing to sacrifice?

- Will you give up your temporary comfort for long term satisfaction?

- Will you give up your need for the approval of others in order to get to   where you want to go?

- Are you willing to make a short time sacrifice for a long term gain?

The memories of your struggles, your uphill battles and miserable journey are fleeting. Once you're past them, just look forward and remember that your circumstances today don't determine what's possible tomorrow.

Let us consider this together, let's say I had a plan to go get groceries in a shop, to check my email when I get back and to work on my project proposal. Just about the time I am about to leave the house, let's say the phone starts ringing and I pick it up. It happens to be a childhood friend going through a situation. I am on the phone with him for a long time, and after our conversation, I realise that time has gone and there is no time for me to do all that I have planned to do. So, I decide to leave everything till the following day. What do you call that? Procrastination! This happens to people all the time. What you are supposed to do today you want to leave it till tomorrow. When tomorrow comes, you want to leave it till the next day.

This situation happens to many people every day with different results. Some people have reasons and excuses while others are unreasonable with themselves and others.

Have you asked yourself this question? How is it that some people succeed when others are left behind figuring it out? Those people who are left behind lack the ability to move past their own excuses. In every situation, there are choices that can be made to further what you are up to in every area of life. When you are focused and have a plan, there are no excuses or reasons that will keep you from achieving that which you have set out to achieve.

A person who has no focus or plan is prone to excusing themselves and others for what has or has not happened. Lack of focus and plan equals excuses and reasons.

What are you willing to do to get what you really want in life?

It is a great question and it seems that the answer should be really simple. But it isn't. In fact, the best way to start figuring out what you are willing to do is by finding out what you are not ready to do. When we are faced with problem or probably when we are in pain, we tend to say we are ready to do anything. And by anything, I mean anything that will make the pain go away. But when the pain is no longer there, we now change the tone from we are ready to do anything to something else. What exactly are you ready to do for that pain which you are facing to go away, in order to have the life of your dream? Would you be ready to quit your job, would you be ready to get new friends, would you be ready to sell your house, would you be ready to invest your savings, would you be ready to eat differently, or change how you spend your spare time? So many people say yes, they can do this, they can do that, but in reality we are not ready to do most of these things. Just by going through these few possibilities, you probably realise that there are things in your life that you really don't want to change. But what if you knew that to have what you really want that was exactly what you had to do? Would you do it?

How about this question: Is the thing you don't want to change bringing you happiness now?

If it isn't, why wouldn't you want to change it? It is like that analogy of cat and dog. Our wants in life are insatiable. You have a dog, but you prefer a cat. When you have a cat, you want a dog. For you to be able to have a dog and have a cat, you have to work towards having both at once. We want everything good for ourselves but how do we go around having those things? Do you know for you to be able to have the dog you may have to get rid of the cat? And for you to be able to have the cat you have to get rid of the dog? I am not saying you should kill the dog or kill the cat. I am saying, do away with one. But are we ready to do that? Most people are not ready to do this. You are not ready to live your comfort zone to be able to achieve what you want in life. I will like to give an example of this.

Once upon a time, there was a woman called Sandra, even though she didn't have a sweet relationship with her husband, the last thing she wanted to do was end the relationship because she was in agony. But she turned herself inside out trying to make things work, pretending that if she just tried harder, somehow that cat was going to turn miraculously into a dog and she would be happy. It is an analogy. She was absolutely willing to do anything to be happy; anything to make that soul-tearing pain go away; She was willing to do anything to stop her pain except leaving the situation that was causing the problem. Can you imagine that? Do you know what is causing your problem? For you to be able to get rid of what is causing your problem, you must be ready to make some changes.

How then can you change what is happening to you? You know your problem already. What you should be thinking of is the solution. Get rid of what is causing you problem, so that you will be able to enjoy your life. But most people are not ready to do it. Think of a situation right now that is causing you pain or confusion and ask yourself these two questions:

What am I willing to do to get out of the pain?

What am I not ready to do?

It is terrifying when you feel like your life has no purpose or direction, but finding your passion can change all that. Finding your passion is like finding your personal road map. When you know what your passion is, you feel motivated, inspired, and so much clearer about what your next step should be.

Ways to Discover Your Passion and work on your dream

1. Slow down.

When we slow down, we are able to tap into the best version of ourselves, which is most often when we find the answers we've been searching for. This might mean practicing yoga, going for daily walks, or setting aside time each day to meditate. Slowing down allows you to quiet the outside voices and listen to yourself.

2. Change your story.

We all tell ourselves stories about who we are, what we're capable of, and what we deserve. If we can identify our self-limiting stories (I'm not good enough; I don't deserve to be happy, etc.), then we can begin writing new stories that are grounded in confidence and courage, and map out actions that move us from one to the other.

3. Own your uniqueness.

We are here for a reason. No one else has your unique blend of talents, wisdom, strengths, skills, and creativity. We all have something great to offer, and learning to accept and own what makes you unique is crucial to sharing your gifts with the world.

4. Cultivate confidence.

If we are continually telling ourselves we can't, then we will never believe we can. There is a chance you may fail, but it will be impossible to succeed if you don't believe in yourself. You can create affirmations, focus on the things you want, or make a vision board that shows your future success.

5. Find the themes.

Recognising the recurring themes in our lives creates a pattern for us to either follow or change. What themes or lessons seem to constantly surface in your life? What are you drawn to again and again? What areas of life seem to be full of discomfort and pain? What areas are full of joy and light?

6. Write.

Ideas flow more freely when we write without an agenda. New inspiration may appear unexpectedly and it becomes easier to connect the dots. Spend a few minutes of quality time each day with a pen and paper allowing yourself to process your thoughts without influence from the outside world.

7. Focus on the fun.

Too often we get wrapped up in the expectations we set for ourselves. We focus on the details and the to-do lists instead of what is most important. What do you love to do? What makes you smile? If money were limitless, what would you be doing today?

8. Push past fear.

It's so seductive to tell ourselves that we'll go after what we want when we have more experience, more money, or more time, but the truth is, that will never happen. We must identify these excuses as masks for our fear. It's only when we get clear on our fears and recognise how it is holding us back that we can begin moving forward.

CHAPTER 2

TAKE ACTION

Most of us are hesitant to start anything because we are afraid we might make mistake or fail. Go ahead make mistakes! Don't wait for more experience or to be good enough to start. You don't have to be good enough to start, but you have to start to be good.

Some may tease and laugh at you. They will warn you, and recite all the reasons why you should not take the risk. These will be the ones to wait around patiently hoping to say "I told you so" Brush them off. If you let these people influence your decision in any way, you will never, ever be ready to go ahead and start making your dream a reality.

You will never have enough money, enough time, enough support, or experience to start. But once you muster up the courage to take the giant step forward and start, the rest will fall in place. But only you can make it happen. Start now with whatever you know, whatever you have and whatever you are.

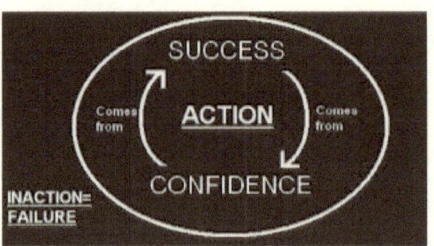

With respect to goals, projects, and other to-do items, it's easy to get stuck too long in the thinking and planning phase. You can sit around writing and rewriting your goals, delving into your subconscious mind, working through emotional blocks, summoning the power of Thor... whatever. But if you don't eventually get into action, you're wasting your time.

How can you get into a sustainable mode of direct action without feeling like you have to torture yourself to get moving? What can you do to cross the barrier between merely thinking about what you want and actually making it happen with your own two hands?

Here's a simple technique I use. This has worked very well for me when I've applied it. It usually takes only 5-10 minutes.

Thought waves

Imagine your thoughts as energy waves that radiate out into the cosmos and then reflect back to you. If your thoughts are chaotic, the waves will interfere with each other, so you probably won't even notice them. But if you put a lot of energy into a single coherent thought, the reflected wave will be strong enough that you'll feel it in your body. At this point you can actually "surf" the wave. When you're surfing your own reflected thought waves, you're in a state of direct action, but it feels effortless. Instead of pushing yourself to act, you're riding a wave of energy that is actually pushing you.

It isn't difficult to create a strong thought wave and then ride it. You do this all the time whenever a powerful thought takes hold of you. For example, when you become really angry, it can be harder to stop yourself than to ride that anger into action. Or when you get a song stuck in your head, you may have a hard time preventing yourself from singing it out loud.

You can also create these thought waves consciously and deliberately. Then you can ride their energy to complete many tasks very quickly. You'll enjoy it too.

How to create and ride thought waves

Sit quietly in a place where you won't be distracted. Take a few deep breaths to clear your mind. Now identify whatever goal you'd like to work on. Maybe it's something simple like organising your workspace or writing a school paper. Or it could be something more complicated like creating a web site for a new online business, moving to a new city, or doubling your income. All you need is a clear, specific, measurable goal, but you don't need a plan of action at this point.

Now just sit and think about what you want. Imagine this goal becoming real. Let yourself daydream, but try to stay conscious as you do it. Explore the goal in your mind. Think about it actually happening, but don't physically try to do anything yourself yet.

For example, if your goal is to switch to a new career, then imagine yourself in that new career right now. Think about what it would be like to actually do that kind of work. Picture yourself doing the work and enjoying it. See the people you're working with, and hold imaginary conversations with them.

Usually within 5-10 minutes, these positive thoughts build up so much energy in my body that I'm itching to do something. At first it feels good just to think about the goal, but eventually I start to feel a tension to get into motion. I can feel the thought energy reflecting back to me. Now it's time to pull out the virtual surfboard and catch the wave.

This is essentially a process of arousal. If you think about sex for a little while, your body will physically respond. Blood will flow to different body parts, for example. If you hold those thoughts long enough, you'll start feeling a compulsion to act on those feelings. Maybe you'll have to take care of yourself or go jump your partner.

You can create a similar type of arousal when fantasizing about your goals. Within a few minutes, you should be noticing different physical sensations in your body – IF your goal is attractive enough to you. Extra blood may even flow to your brain and muscles, preparing you for action.

Once you start feeling that positive tension in your body, stop and ask yourself this question:

Take action

What can I do right now to make this goal a reality?

As you ask this question, hold the expectation that the answer will be something simple that can be done in 30 minutes or less.

Whatever reasonable answer pops into your head, accept it and act on it immediately. At this point you should find it very easy to take action — it would be harder to procrastinate. Do you procrastinate on sex when you're physically aroused?

Now you've caught the energy wave. The next trick is to ride it as far as you can before it eventually dissipates.

Get that simple task done as quickly as you can. Sometimes you'll flow effortlessly into another task. But if you don't know what to do next, that's no problem. Just stop again and ask yourself:

What can I do right now to make this goal a reality?

Accept whatever idea comes to you next, and get it done. Keep repeating this question and taking action for as long as you can. I'll usually go about 2-4 hours without a break, sometimes much longer. In this state I can quickly plough through many different tasks. It feels good too.

It may take a little practice to build up the energy in your body and then release it gradually. Your ability to use this technique will surely improve over time.

Whether or not you achieve your goals is often largely up to what *you* do to make them happen. So make sure that you are actively and consistently working to achieve them, and that you don't let others determine whether you are successful or not.
However, in order for this to work, you must first make sure that your goals truly reflect what *you* want to achieve, and are not primarily a function of other's wishes or expectations for you.

The following consideration will help....

Be in Charge

Think of your goals often and keep them in mind when making decisions in your life, even those that don't seem directly related to your goal. For example, making a decision about whether to move in with your girlfriend may not seem directly relevant to your goal to finish college, but if she is not very supportive of this goal, moving in with her could make it more difficult for you to do so.

Develop necessary skills.

You are much more likely to be successful in your goals if you have developed a skill set that will help you to achieve them, and if you have confidence in your ability to use those skills to achieve that goal. So, for example, if you have a relationship goal of reducing the amount of conflict and anger in your romantic relationship, it would be very helpful to learn some basic skills of effective communication.

Seek out support.

Having the support of significant others in our lives -- friends, family members or romantic partners -- can significantly increase the chances that we'll achieve our goals. That support can come in the form of tangible help, like when your partner takes care of the household chores so that you can study for a midterm. But just as important is emotional support. Getting encouragement from those close to us, or even just a caring ear willing to listen to our concerns, can be really helpful, especially when trying to accomplish challenging goals.

Why is it important to seek out support?

When a goal is supported by significant others in your life, your motivation to accomplish the goal may be higher. And, of course, the support that you receive may actually help you to achieve your goal. For example, if you reach out to your parents for support while obtaining the goal of getting a college degree.

That said, having people around us who are *not* supportive of our goals, or who, even worse, actively demean them or discourage us from pursuing them can be really harmful to our success. So watch out! Try to minimize their negative impact on your life. Don't let their negativity colour the way you see yourself. It's not a bad thing to seek the suggestions of friends and family members around you. It is only wise to sieve the suggestions given to you before you act. Remember, you are 100% responsible for the action you take.

Too many people stroll passively through life, intrigued by a whole slew of possibilities but not committed to making any of them a reality.

What is the difference between interest and commitment? Do you know?

- Interest reads a blog post, commitment applies that post day after day
- Interest works an hour a day on your business; commitment works whenever time permits
- Interest procrastinates; commitment focuses on what is important

- Interest makes excuses; commitment constantly acquires new skills and solutions.

If you are struggling with this issue, ask yourself this question. What am i holding back? What is stopping me from living the life i have imagined for myself?

If you want it bad enough, if you are committed, you will find a way to make it happen. If the thought of slaving away in a cubicle for the rest of your life is a powerful enough motivation for you to work tirelessly in order to escape it, i will advise you to go for it.

The biggest complaint i hear is this: "I would take action and get started , but i just don't know enough yet. I am just not ready yet."

To this, I have two suggestions:

1. **There is always more to learn.** The amount of information on the internet is equivalent to a stack of books stretching from Earth to Pluto 10 times! If you keep waiting until you finish that book, podcast or video course, if you keep waiting until you are ready, you will never be ready.
2. **You learn far more from experience than consumption**. I learned more during my first book launch than I did during the prior 6 months of ravenous information consumption. Concepts are introduced via information; skills are honed through action.

I am not saying you should blindly act for the sake of action, not at all. In fact, if you want to be successful, learning must be a continual process. After all, it is hard to create value if you don't know what you are talking about.

The key is to distinguish between the kind of compulsive, ineffective learning that so many marketers struggle with and learning for the sole purpose of taking action. Don't wait to get started. Start now and correct your course as you go along.

Are you ready to go all out? Are you ready to throw off the bowlines and fully commit yourself to achieving a life of freedom and adventure?

If so, here is what to do...

1. **GET YOUR MINDSET RIGHT**

   Success in any aspect of life starts with your mindset. Faulty beliefs and assumptions are like powerful headwinds halting your progress and blowing you off course. In order to truly "go all out" and make unprecedented progress, you must make the decision at a core level to hold nothing back. You must take a good look at your life and decide that nothing is going to stand in your way of success. This kind of raw, unrestrained dedication is extremely powerful and it works.

2. **REFINE YOUR GOALS**

   It is hard to commit yourself to something if your finish line is just a nebulous point off in the distance. So before you do anything, get ruthlessly clear about what your ultimate outcome looks like.. Nail down exactly what you want, how you are going to get there and on what sort of timeline you plan to reach your destination.

3. **FOCUS ON WHAT IS IMPORTANT**

   While the right mindset will give you the motivation you need to bring your A game, if you focus on unimportant activities you still aren't going to get anywhere! Going for it" doesn't mean quadrupling your workload. Work for the sake of work is not the goal. The goal is to live and work on your own terms. This is especially significant if you already have a busy life full of responsibilities. In order to achieve freedom and escape the trap of selling your time for money, you must be ruthlessly selective about what you work on and what you ignore.

4. HOLD YOURSELF ACCOUNTABLE

Unfortunately, personal drive usually isn't enough. It may be enough to get you started, but after a week or two, the "new year resolution effect" begins to set in and your initial enthusiasm slowly begins to fade. In order to stay committed, you need a way of holding yourself accountable.

How? Here are my top 3 ways:

- **Use the weekly goal system** to keep track of your most important tasks. At the beginning of each week, write down your top goals for the next 7 days. Before you go to bed each night, write down 2-3 key tasks that , if accomplished, will leave you satisfied with your day. Once you complete your goals for the day, stop guilt free.
- **Tell others what you are doing.** At the very least, tell your family about the goals you are trying to reach. Even if their reactions are less than supportive, getting your ambitions out in the open will help you stay committed.
- **Join a community.** Surrounding yourself with like-minded people who are rooting for (and expecting) your success can be extremely powerful. It can provide you with the confidence and motivation you need to take your dream to a whole new level.

If you have been putting off anything in life , i invite you to ask yourself why. What are you waiting for?

If you have been waiting for the stars to align in your favour, if you have been waiting for that perfect moment to arrive... I have got news for you:

It will never come.

Take action

There will always be a new problem standing in your way. Something you need to do before you can fully commit yourself.

CHAPTER 3

BELIEF IN YOURSELF

Did you ever find yourself in a situation where you saw someone just becoming successful or achieve a certain breakthrough and you thought to yourself: "I can never do that"? Most of us probably have. This is the result of something called, self-limiting beliefs that have been rooted in your mind.

What are self-limiting beliefs?

Self-limiting beliefs are mental blocks, negative thoughts, psychological hindrances or inner monsters stored in your mind. They tend to have a negative effect on you and they greatly limit your ability and programme your mind to discard all possibilities of ever achieving your goals and ultimately your success.

There are numerous definitions of self-limiting beliefs, but in this book, I will touch on the six top ones that I personally feel, have the worst effect on people.

Let's explore them together:

* Believing that you are not good enough to achieve anything: This probably starts from the fact that you first thought that you are not smart enough, have no special abilities or qualities. And since you don't have them, then you are not worthy or you can't achieve anything great.

* Believing that people don't generally like you: Before I tackle this, I need you to understand that I am explaining this in terms of normal, natured and perhaps even a well-mannered person. And not in terms of a rude, insensitive or bad mannered person who deserves to be hated by people. This belief leads you to think that no one likes you or wants to be your friend because of your flaw or flaws. You generally accept that you will never be liked, hence stamped the belief in your mind.

* Believing that you will be rejected: This is a very common self-limiting belief which exists in many different types of individuals from different walks of life. It exists in a student who is fearful of asking a teacher for assistance, a worker asking a colleague for help and even children asking their parents for certain things because they don't want to be refused.

* Believing that certain tasks are impossible to achieve: It's prudent to know here that, I am not talking about universally or psychologically impossible tasks to achieve, such as; humans flying, a child being older than her parents or a fan being on and off at the same time. Rather, the tasks I am focusing on are those that have been proven time and time again to be very possible to be achieved. Yet, people with this belief, limit themselves by saying they simply cannot achieve these tasks because they lack the qualities, knowledge, tools, resources and so on.

* Having one side track belief: People with this thought believe that there is one solution to a particular equation, or simply put, there is only one way to perform a certain task or to do things. After trying the only way they know and it doesn't work for them, they will back out. They don't want to explore. They don't want an alternative. They don't have a plan B. They are just one sided.

* Believing that you are destined for failure: It will surprise you to know that there are people like that around. This is one of the most damaging self-limiting beliefs anyone can possess. Sadly, it exists in a huge percentage among us. People with this belief deeply believe that whatever they do, they will end up in failure. And because of this, they don't set out to try anything beneficial or they stop half way when they are faced with circumstances or situations. Limiting beliefs are usually formed in the very early stages of life. It starts when you are exposed to a new situation or new environment and your first experience in that situation is negative or unpleasant. If it were a one off occurrence, then it will not form your limiting belief. However, if you keep experiencing negative and unpleasant results in the same situation and environment, then you are going to start doubting yourself. You are going to start wondering if others are doing the right thing and what you are doing is wrong. As time goes on and you experience more negative results, the frequency which is increased by the doubts you already have, your doubt starts to grow stronger and stronger until it reaches the point where it becomes rock- solid belief that would have become deeply rooted in your mind. It has become part of your identity.

At this point, it's basically like you have no free will; you are a slave to your confrontation. It's going to take time and repetition of you proving your limiting beliefs wrong. The more you prove your limiting belief wrong, the weaker it becomes, until it eventually fades away and has no power over you anymore. The bonus is that, once your limiting belief starts to lose its power over you, you will become much more confident too. This way, the reinforcing circle becomes a positive one. Then your actions boost your confidence, which in turn boosts your result, which boosts your confidence even more, so take them out.

What is that voice in your head saying to you now? Is it telling you something like, you can't do it. You will never be good enough. You are going to fail.

This voice taunts you whenever you set a goal. It criticizes you when life gets difficult. It beats you down when you struggle to stand up against its running commentary.

You know you should not let self-doubt bother you, but it's a sneaky critter. Sometimes, you just can't contain it and it slips past your barriers. Self-doubt is greedy. When it's loose, it devours your confidence, strips logic and reason from your mind, and steals happiness from your heart. In return, it leaves you with only fear and insecurity. The more you fight your self-doubt, the more it fights back. However, with self-knowledge and understanding, you can use self-doubt for your benefit.

When I was a child, i was in love with writing stories. For me, writing stories was as exciting as going to the playground. At some point in my childhood, I decided I had become a Lawyer. But the critics in my life were quick to cut me down. I'll bet you have heard the same clichés.

"Being a Lawyer is great but not a realistic future goal. While it's a nice love writing as an hobby, becoming a Lawyer is a much more difficult and unrealistic dream. You will just be another starving lawyer."

As children, we internalise these negative messages and parrot them back. If the adults say so, it must be true, right? By adulthood, every time we have small hope, we are the first to snuff it out.

"I will never be as good as the real professionals anyway. I don't even have a degree from a well known school. For many years I stopped myself before I even tried. I did that because I was living under the negative colour of the people around me who believe I was not good enough to be a Lawyer. I was afraid of what people would say. I was afraid they would say, "we have told you" I was afraid of failing as a Lawyer.

When fear grabs you, your beloved goal forever feels out of reach. But it doesn't just stop there, does it? If left unchecked, the infectious bite of fear and self-doubt can spread. You unconsciously start questioning your knowledge and abilities in everything you do. And if you are like me, you desperately want to find a cure. One fateful day, I realised that trying to beat out my self-doubt wouldn't rebuild my confidence. If I wanted to believe in myself, I needed to face my self-doubt and be willing to take care of it.

Before, I used to imagined self-doubt as a life-sucking monster. Now, I realised it's actually a fearful, angry and lost creature secretly crying for help.

Like fear, joy and sadness, doubt is part of human nature and it needs understanding. If you want to improve yourself, you need to tame your self-doubt and fight with it. That means paying attention to how you react to things, understanding the root of your insecurities and taking steps to address your fears.

Now I no longer tell myself "I will never be a good Lawyer." Instead, I ask myself "What can I do to become better?" I went for my dream ignoring naysayers who said it would be difficult.

Self-doubt doesn't have to be as monstrous as we make it out to be. It's all about perspective.

The following tips will help you manage your self-doubt

- **Identify and ease your doubts**
  Learning how to recognise when your self-talk takes a turn for the worse is crucial. When you hear yourself saying "I can't," or "I don't know," or "What if", a red flag should go up. Instead of telling yourself "I can't do it," say "I can't do it yet. But i am working on it."
  Or if you start wondering. "What if I fail?" you can respond by saying "Then I will try again." Doing this transforms a negative situation into an opportunity for growth. In the end, it's about giving yourself a chance.

- **Stop listening to toxic people**
  Toxic people are convinced that everything is impossible and they are quick to shoot down ideas. They will poison your mind into a state of hopelessness. Don't let them steal your energy because they have lost theirs. Instead, surround yourself with supportive and passionate people who can both inspire you and bring out the best in you. You can find them among friends, family, even through the books you

read. You need people that will lift you up when you feel down and help you see the bright side of your darkest fears and doubts.

- **Recall your successes**
  This one is tough. Especially when you are down, you will more easily remember the bad instead of the good. Oftentimes, the "rah-rah" pep talk just doesn't cut in.

- Give yourself permission to try ...and try again
  Self-doubt never disappears. Overtime, you just get better at dealing with it. It will greet you every time you fall out of your comfort Zone and whenever you strive to do something great. Your doubts are only thoughts, not your future.
  Sure, something may go wrong. But if you never try, you are losing an opportunity to improve your life

Many times over the years, I have heard a story about how the circle is used to train elephants. I sincerely hope that this practice is historical. The story goes that when a baby elephant was brought into the circle, it was immediately chained to a stick in the ground. As a youngster, the animal is conditioned to only move the distance allowed by the chain. As an enormous strong intelligent adult, the chain is replaced by a rope but the elephant still only moves the distance allowed by the rope because she thinks she is still held back by that strong heavy chain. The adult elephant could easily break the rope and stroll away from her confine, but she doesn't. She is controlled by her conditioning. Oh yes! The chain is now in her mind not on her leg. I encourage you to consider what chains are in your mind causing you not to change your life. This is the key to change, to break free of outdated, untrue and harmful beliefs. The elephant still saw a chain around her ankle, though it was only a rope, a rope she could easily break loose.

What ropes are you seeing in your life as a chain? Are you ready to stretch that rope or maybe, even break it?

Once upon a time, there was a woman whose son had a drug addiction problem. At significant personal financial expense, this woman actually kept a lawyer on retainer because he was always in court for drug related offences. She made excuses to his teachers and later his boss. It was a great inconvenience to her life. She drove him to and from work when he lost his driving licence. She allowed his family into her home, when they were evicted and didn't have anywhere to stay. When this man started stealing her money, she could not tell anybody.

To most of us reading this story, this woman's rope is pretty obvious, "cut it loose", you are probably yelling by now. This woman's perspective was different. In her mind, she didn't see her 27 years old son as an adult. She still saw a frightened, hurting, angry little boy. After several years, and thanks to counselling, coaching and supporting group of parents like her. This woman chose to change how she looked at her son's situation. When she changed, it changed. When she tends to test the strength of the rope of her behaviour which placed her son's needs above her own, she empowered herself and empowered her son to begin taking responsibility for his own life. Eventually, she stopped driving him, so he took the bus to work and he arrived on time. She gave him thirty days to move out of her home, and in that time frame, he found a small apartment for his family. When he was on his own, his mum wasn't constantly checking up on him, telling him to get help. He also sought counsel for his addictive habit. When this woman chose to break free from the old pattern of making everything okay for her son, things became much more okay for her. When she changed the way she looked at things, that is, when she let go of the belief that she was responsible for making her son's life work for him, the things she looked at, changed. She saw that he was an adult making poor choices, partially reinforced by the enabling behaviours. This woman's early behaviour was a chain of outdated beliefs and misplaced guilt.

When she saw that the chain was really a breakable rope, she began to test its strength much to her satisfaction. Her son is now taking responsibility for his life. When you change the way you look at things, the things you look at change. Like this woman, each of us see chains where there are only breakable ropes. I encourage you today to look at that which is stopping you from achieving that which you want to achieve and break loose.

What is the moral of this woman's story?

Human beings are subject to self-limiting beliefs especially during childhood, when most of us genuinely, physically, mentally and emotionally incompetent, knew otherwise. We look up to the adults for emulation and guidance. When limitations are imposed, we tend to view it as a permanent part of our identity. Not realizing that we can overcome limitations. Especially with the proper mind-set, thinking, training and experience.

Change your thought, change your belief, identify what has been holding you back, and challenge them. Hold on to the fact that the belief can be overcome. Breakthrough this limiting belief and change your performance, change your result and change your life.

Once upon a time, there was a little dog that was always chained to a tree for several years when outside of the house. The chain was twenty feet, and the dog would run as far as that twenty feet and stop. This went on for so many years. Finally, the owner of the dog felt sorry for it and removed the chain. The dog would still run twenty feet and stop, even the cat that tormented it for so many years by staying just a few feet away from the chain was safe. The dog will run to the twenty foot mark and just short of the cat and stop, no longer held back by the chain but by the conditioning of its own limiting beliefs. A couple more steps and the dog could have walked through it forever. Just a couple more steps, and so can you. That is the good and exonerating news; we can identify and let go of our limiting beliefs. Are you ready to do that? What is holding you back? Stop seeing the chain. Look at the rope which you can break loose.

Few years ago, I happened to meet a woman at the supermarket who wanted to pursue her life dream of having her own business. She worked for a Group Home as a day provider but wanted to establish a better control of her destiny. She was hesitant to do this. Afraid that she wouldn't be able to make enough money to quit her boring day job, her biggest challenge to succeed was not her ability. It was her belief in herself. This woman had a self-limiting belief. Most of her friends and her acquaintances doubted her ability to be a business owner. They advised her to keep doing that job which was giving her pain. At least, she was able to get some money to pay her rent and look after her daily needs. Fortunately for this woman, she didn't want to totally give up her idea. while she continued to have a nagging doubt about what she wanted to do, her goal was totally supported by a new business acquaintance. Her business acquaintance gave her encouragement, made time available whenever she needed questions or suggestions, or just to talk about business issues.

 Although, she had the right plan and ability to succeed, she remained her own worst obstacle. The good news is that she continued even though she struggled with self-doubts, but persevered and quit her day job eventually. What she conquered was much more than issues around developing her business. She conquered her own apprehension, her own self-doubt. She succeeded because she didn't listen to the naysayers. She succeeded because she overcame the greatest obstacle, her unbelief in herself.

You want to go out and do something, but you are so scared to leave your comfort zone. This happens to so many people. Because something is happening to you, you love it where you are. You don't want to step out into the world unknown. Successful people take risks. You must be ready to step into the world unknown for you to be able to achieve what you want to achieve.

This woman in the story actually wanted something good for herself. She wanted to have her own business. But she was filled with her self- limiting beliefs, scared that she wouldn't be able to handle it. Those she turned to for advice discouraged her . Instead of lifting her up, they said things which would make her remain where she was. They said: "Stay where you are and continue to suffer in silence". You have people like that around you.

How do you remove your self-limiting beliefs?

- Identify the fact that you have it in you. You need to know exactly what thoughts and beliefs you have that have stopped you from being happy and from reaching your goals. For example, are you happy with your present financial situation? If not, then, why not? Is it because you believe it's hard to make money? Is it because you believe that you are not smart enough to have your own business? Is it because you believe you can't get a better job? All of these I have mentioned are limiting beliefs.

- Once you have identified your limiting beliefs; in all areas of your life: business, dating, social, health and so on, then you can start working on how to remove them. I can't stress enough how important it is to observe yourself and try to identify your limiting beliefs. Everyone has at least one, but some people have dozens. I used to have so many limiting beliefs. And I have slowly walked my way through them. I still have limiting beliefs today, and whenever I discover one, I immediately work on removing it.

- Personally, I found that the best way to remove a limiting belief is to prove that it is irrational and fake. You do this with corporate proofs and logical evidence. Find examples of people who have achieved what your limiting belief is telling you is not possible. If you think you are poor because you are dump and don't have a degree, then make it your mission to find three or more people without a degree who are making a lot of money. If you are massively overweight and you think it's impossible to get into shape, and become healthy, find three or more people who used to be overweight and managed to *get slim*. By doing this, you prove to yourself that your limiting belief is exactly what you think it is. Now, you can say to yourself, "If They can do it, so can I". Think about this.

Keep in mind that you can do whatever you set out to do, what you just need to do is to work positively towards doing it. If they could do it, you as well can do it. Who says you cannot be a good actor? Who says you cannot be a good singer? Who says you cannot own your own business? You can do all these things by changing your mind-set from something negative to something positive.

What is holding you back?

Stop focusing on those who were not able to do it. Those people decided to quit because they didn't know how to pursue their dream. Look out for successful people who have been able to do that thing and they did it successfully.

Are You Determined To Fail?

Do you notice the theme the question above? There is an undercurrent of self–doubt and vulnerability. The unspoken thought that drives these question is, "I don't believe these ideas will work for me." Or, stated another way, "I don't believe I can make these ideas work. I don't believe in myself."

Worrying about not being able to implement a few diet changes is just one tiny example of this fear. But a lack of belief in yourself will limit you no matter how great the ideas or opportunities are that you are exposed to.

My biggest question to you is this: Why are you determined to make these ideas *not* work for you? Why are you searching for reasons why these ideas won't succeed instead of figuring out a way to make something good happen?

The biggest difference between successful people and unsuccessful ones (in health, in business, and in life) is that successful people are determined to make the situation work for them rather than playing the role of the victim and searching for reasons why a situation won't work.

No idea will work for every person on the planet, but many ideas can work for most people … if you believe that you can make them work. You have to be willing to not just think differently, but to also experiment with new ideas and trust that you'll discover a way to make them work.

The biggest difference I've noticed between successful people and unsuccessful people isn't intelligence or opportunity or resources. It's the belief that they can make their goals happen.

We all deal with vulnerability, uncertainty, and failure. Some of us trust that if we move forward anyway, then we will figure it out.

Do You Believe That Change Is Possible for You?

One of the most foundational beliefs of this community is that you can become better.

We believe that it is possible for human beings to improve. We believe that it is possible to raise the bar in your own life even if the world around you accepts average. We believe in ourselves and in each other. We believe that if you want better health or more happiness or a more meaningful job that you can make those things happen.

And because of this belief we are willing to test, experiment, and try new things even when we feel uncertain. If you don't believe that it's possible to make new things work, then it's hard to make any progress. I don't care how good the ideas are, nothing will work for you if you don't believe in it. And more importantly, nothing will work if you don't believe in yourself.

Not everyone can achieve their dream in this world, that's because most people have sentimental attachments that keeps them from making the tough decisions that are necessary to get to the ultimate top, while down there they keep on believing what most of us hold on to when we have nothing else to say, words like God has better plans for you in the future keeps hanging in there. Let me ask you something when your life is a living hell how can you hold on to a tip of a sharp sword? the only person who has and can make better plans for you is no one but you, look deep past what you see, the world is suffering, don't be so blind to plant a tree on a desert where water doesn't exist, you can be a miracle the moment you believe in you and awaken your spirit and take part on something that you believe in, there's a vast land around you to do or become something, don't wait for rain to come, while you can reign your world, in life, you get what you put in, remember life is happening right now.

Instead of dwelling on the past or worrying about the future, or waiting on a promise that you have no idea when it's going to come, practice being and living in the present moment, right now is the only moment guaranteed to you. Right now is life. Don't miss it, don't miss a thing just because you're stressed. How you feel when you're stressed is not a true measure of reality. Just because you're afraid, doesn't mean you're in danger. Just because you feel alone, doesn't mean nobody loves you. Just because you think you might fail, doesn't mean you will. Look beyond your doubts and keep searching for the truth. Be aware of your mental self-talk. We all talk silently to ourselves in our heads, but we aren't always conscious of what we're saying or how it's affecting us. The way to overcome negative thoughts and destructive emotions is to develop opposing, positive emotions that are stronger and more powerful. Listen to your self-talk and replace negative thoughts with positive ones.

The sun is always shining on some part of your life. Sometimes you just have to forget how you feel, remember what you deserve, and keep pushing forward, do what you must do to get things done. All roads leads to somewhere and often not to where we are heading, wherever the road might take you, be you and do something that your future self-will thank you for, don't be negative every time something bad happens to you and fail to achieve your goal, someday you may achieve that you cry for today, and few days later you will not be happy and dream another dream and embark to conquer it. Don't stress yourself to find happiness, have a peace of mind, just like the world goes in a circle, so things in our life will come and go but we must remain at peace in our hearts and in our minds.

Happiness is never constant, and it's not supposed to be. – You have to fight through some bad days to earn the best days of your life. To believe that you can reach a state of happiness and stay there forever, is like the tide believing she can reach for the shoreline and remain there forever; or like a fruit tree believing that if she only holds on tighter, she can keep her fruit from dropping to the ground. Happiness is simply a series of moments that come and go and add sweetness to our lives. Learn to accept this, and the more happy moments you will have. Many of us compete in a race then when we come short of achieving our goals, we start hating everything. Failures are temporary situations that teach us necessary lessons. – Life's best lessons are usually learned at the worst times and from the worst mistakes. So yes, you will fail sometimes. The faster you accept this, the faster you can get on with being brilliant. You'll never be 100% sure it will work, but you can always be 100% sure doing nothing won't work.

Doing something and getting it wrong is at least ten times more productive than doing nothing. So get out there and try! Either you succeed or you learn a vital lesson. Win – Win. Don't be so bitter to accept your results, there's nothing you can do now to undo them, but go back to training, and train harder and smarter. One thing I've learned about life is you cannot always be a winner. You may not be where you want to be yet, but if you think about it, you're no longer where you once were either. You have good reason to believe that you can trust yourself going forward. Not because you've always made the right choices, but because you survived the bad ones, and taken small steps in the right direction. So cry for a moment if you have to, and get it out of your system. Crying doesn't indicate that you're weak; since birth, it has always been a sign that you're alive and full of potential. Once you're done, keep going! You're undoubtedly getting closer to where you want to be. Live a simple life far from crazy expectation, but only daring to push your limits when the strength is in you. You can get better, but life never gets any better, only your perception of it does. The world around you changes when you change. If you awake every morning with the thought that something wonderful will happen in your life today, and you pay close attention, you'll often find that you're right. The opposite is also true. The choice is yours to make. Believe in you, and not just try to give your best but do better than your best in what you, and something best for you will unfold. I've always believed that positive thinking is at the forefront of every great success story. for instance for us Kenyan runners we don't have quit in us, for where we come from it's a disgrace for you have let down the name of your country, your training mates, your family, your manager, your coach and above to yourself. Before I run, I like to visualize what I'm going to do, I make it better in my mind according to how I'm feeling so I will not get ahead of myself, this mentality has helped me on my everyday life, like at work, some days I have six or nine clients to massage in a day, yet I will go with no food but only water, tea and milk, it's not like I'm torturing myself but I only eat when I'm hungry not when I think about it, my inner self-will tell me when its hungry, most of us Kenyan runners have fought, survive and endured many things in our live, those things that we have face has shape us to be strong even in the life beyond our realm. When you give your spirit the power to control your life, you can do more than you ever thought you are capable off. Before doing something take time to visualize it, do it mentally before you do it physically. The mind must believe it can do something before it is capable of actually doing it. The way to overcome negative thoughts and destructive emotions is to develop opposing, positive emotions that are stronger and more powerful. Listen to your self-talk and replace negative thoughts with positive ones. Regardless of how a situation seems, focus on the next positive step forward

CHAPTER 4

EXPECT FAILURE

A lot of us are afraid to fail. We believe it as a sign of weakness and can even come to regret ever taking that leap of faith. Well, contrary to this belief, a number of highly successful achievers often credit a failure or two, to their success.

The fact is that mistakes and failure are a part of life. Instead of fearing them, why not make it okay to make mistakes and to fail? Why not take the onus off of failure? Why not embrace the process of learning and growing instead of only being focused on the outcome of your efforts? Why not focus on enjoying the process of learning and creating something that is important to you?

People who don't worry about success or failure, who instead are excited about their learning and growing process, generally find their way to succeed. The reason for this is that they don't let failure stop them. Instead, failure spurs them on to work harder, to put forth even more effort to learn what they need to learn to succeed.

On the other hand, even very smart people, who are dominated by their ego wounded selves, generally allow failure to derail them. Believing they are a failure if they fail, they become too afraid to make more effort. In addition, they often believe that success or failure is not dependent on effort, but on ability. When this is their belief, they often give up at the first sign of failure, fearing that, if their natural intelligence and ability is not leading to success, then there is no point in trying harder.

Creating Success

Every successful person knows that effort, creativity, openness to learning, and perseverance are what create success, not necessarily high intelligence, talent, or ability. Every truly successful person is someone who has not allowed failure to stop him or her from forging ahead with passion and purpose.

Failure is a type of freedom. Why? Because the worst has happened. Now, you can relax and rebuild your life. You do not have to fail on a large scale, but failure in life is inevitable. There is no way to live life without failing from time to time. The only way you won't fail is if you live so guardedly that you are barely living at all, wherein, you fail by default. A wise thinker once stated, "Avoiding danger is no safer in the long run than out-and-out exposure, and the fearful are captured just as frequently as the bold." Failure is not something to shun, but something to embrace.

The Importance of Failure

Okay, it's clear; we all will face failures in life. However, this does not mean we should *"chase failure"* in order to get it over with, so to speak. It's a funny thing, but failure is never planned. It's the companion of success. An unwanted companion for sure, but nevertheless, a very important one.
When we resist failure, it attaches itself to us. You don't solve an issue by resisting it. We overcome failure by accepting it, analyzing it, dissecting it, and looking at it from every possible angle. Without failure, there is no growth.
 Success is based on going from failure to failure without losing eagerness."
Of course, some individuals are sardonic. These types of people never pick themselves up from failure because they did not grow from a previous failure. Failure is the most wonderful teacher if we are willing to learn from it.

Success does not come easy. Everyone must face one hurdle after another. It's the only way to reach success. The reason being is that success must be maintained. If you think that once you have the success you crave and it's time to relax, you are sadly mistaken. For example, you've always wanted to buy a home. You finally purchase the home of your dreams. However, your home must be maintained. Once a goal is reached, you must have the tenacity to remain there and move higher if you wish. Without repeated failures, you do not have the know-how of sustainability.

Even though success is the power that hastens us en route to our goals, it is failure that guides us to those goals that count. When failure is acknowledged as being just as vital as success, it's easier to accept it freely and carry on with searching for a resolution.

A very well known fellow stated, *"the most successful people are those who are good at Plan B."* Individuals who are good at "brushing failure off their shoulders" take the necessary steps to try again, usually with Plan B. In fact, Plan B may not even be a plan at all! Plan B is the *"I can do it attitude."* Plan B, is the transition from failure to success. We can comprehend the function for failure if we acknowledge that human beings prefer to "dispel the uneasiness of failure." Human beings are forever determined to achieve their loftiest goals as frequently as time permits. However, failure surrounds us and no person ever experiences a total lack of uneasiness. There is always that smidgen of the unknown. Regardless of our best efforts, we are never 100% sure of success! There is always that lingering doubt in the back of our minds; in spite of this, our will is stronger than failure and doubt inevitably loses.

"The desire to succeed, must be great than the fear of failure." This statement was made by well-known actor and comedian Bill Cosby. In our personal and professional lives, the aforementioned quote states the significance of failure and how big a part it plays in each of our lives. Consider this. During the day, where is your energy focused? Is it focused on succeeding or failing? Is the glass half-empty or half full? Our thoughts have us on leash. Eventually, we go where they lead.

If you focus on negativity, then your world become cynical. If you focus on positivism, even the harshest defeat is only a stepping-stone. A mother was speaking with her daughter who was despondent about repeated failures. She spoke about well-known personalities and how they succeeded because they "tried that one last time." This gave her daughter the incentive to try again. After reading about the importance of failure she stated, "you never know what waits beyond failure; therefore, I will try again." Failure is the stratagem that leads to success. Without it, where would we be?

All stories of success are also stories of great failures. But, people don't see failures. They only see one side of the picture and they say, "That person got lucky. He must have been at the right place at the right time".

I have lots of names in my list. I will share some with you. There was a man who failed in business at the age of twenty one, he was defeated in a legislative race at the age of twenty two, he failed again in business at the age of twenty four, he overcame the death of his sweet heart at the age of twenty six, he had a nervous breakdown at the age of twenty seven, he lost a congressional race at the age of thirty four, he lost a senatorial race at the age of thirty five, he failed in an effort to become vice president at the age of forty seven, he lost a senatorial race at the age of forty nine, and he was elected President of the United States at the age of fifty two. Do you know this man? This man was Abraham Lincoln. Would you call him a failure? No. He could have quit you know. But this man refused to quit because he had a dream. It's the same with all successful people. Regardless of how many times they failed, they will still continue to fight. The major difference between successful people and those who are struggling with their dream is in their persistence. The fact that you have tried it so many times and didn't get it right doesn't mean you are a failure. You will only be a failure if you quit trying.

Another example is Oprah Winfrey. Most people know Oprah as one of the most iconic faces on T.V. as well as one of the richest and most successful women in the world. Oprah faced a hard time to get to that position. Oprah was actually sacked by her employer because they said she was not fit to appear on T.V. Oprah decided to turn this around. She worked on her weakness and she was able to do that which they said she could not do. She worked on that weakness and she was able to turn it to her advantage.

Another good example is Winston Churchill. Winston Churchill was twice elected as the Prime Minister of the United Kingdom. But could you believe that Churchill actually failed the sixth grade when he was in school? After school, he faced many years of political failures as he was defeated in every election for public office. But he finally became the Prime Minister at the age of sixty two. Picture somebody who failed sixth grade. He tried severally to be elected and he failed severally. He refused to give up. He looked at himself and he said he wanted something. He worked positively towards that which he wanted.

That you are doing it or you have done it so many times and it's not working and people are mocking you, is not enough reason for you to say you want to stop trying it. If you stop trying, it will only confirm what they have said about you, that you are a failure.

Another wonderful example is Soichiro Honda. We may be familiar with Honda Motors. They are everywhere, from cars to motor cycles. But do you know the real story of how challenging it was for Soichiro Honda to establish Honda Motors? I will tell you. Like most other countries, Japan was hit badly by the great depression of the 1930s. In 1938, Soichiro Honda was still in school when he started the little workshop developing the concept of the piston-ring. His plan was to sell this idea to Toyota. He laboured night and day. He even slept in the workshop, always believing that he could perfect the design and produce a worthy product.

At that time, he was married. When he was short of cash, he asked his wife whether he could sell her Jewellery. The wife agreed and they sold her Jewellery to continue with the design. When it was produced, he took this design to Toyota. Only for that design to be turned down because Toyota Motors said the standard was quite below their own standard. Think about this. After spending your time, your money, you sold your property to produce something because you believed that the product was going to give you something wonderful in life. It was going to be your breakthrough. You now took that product to where you are meant to supply it, only to be turned down. You are told that it was below their standard. Some people would give up.

But this man, even though he was mocked by his friends, and in debt, refused to give up. He went back to redesign the product, he then took it back again to Toyota. But this time, it was accepted because it was just exactly what they wanted. You can do the same thing. How do you see yourself? That is what I am saying about being persistent. This man refused to give up. Is that the end of the story for this man? No! I will tell you more about him. After the product had been accepted by Toyota, he was asked to supply them. So he needed a factory which he could use to supply Toyota. He decided to build a factory. He was able to gather materials together and built the factory. Upon completing the factory, do you know what happened to this man? He was faced with another situation; a very strong problem, because this factory was burnt twice. It's enough for anybody to say, "You know what, I think this is enough for me". This man refused to quit. He continued and he said to himself he was going to do it. Do you know why this man refused to quit? It is because he believed so much in himself. He did not let the distractions of the naysayers to stop him from working on his dream.

In life, people dream and they want something good. They want to work towards what they want in life. But when they are faced with situations, they give up. There is no way one can avoid facing problems in life, especially when you are working on the road to success. As you are working to get something done, you will face obstacles, you will face problem, you will face situations. The way you handle your problem will determine the outcome you will get. This man refused to give up. Soichiro Honda started collecting surplus gasoline can discarded by U.S fighters who were fighting wars at that time. This was what he used to build the new factory. After the war, an extreme gasoline shortage forced people to walk or use bicycle. Honda built a fighting engine and attached it to his bicycle. His neighbours wanted the same thing. Although he tried, materials could not be found and he was unable to supply his neighbours. Was it the end of the road for him? No! Soichiro refused to give up.

He wrote inspiring letters to eighteen thousand shops of bicycle owners, asking them to help him revitalise Japan. Five thousand people responded by giving him money to support his ideas. Unfortunately for him, the first models were too bulky to work well. So he continued to develop and adapt until finally the small engine which he named "Super Cub", became a reality and was a success. With success in Japan, Honda began exporting his bicycle engines to Europe and America.

Was that the end of the story? No! In the 1970s, there was another gas shortage. This time in America, automotive fashion turned to small cars. Honda was paid to be on the trend because they were now experts in building small engine cars. The companies started making tiny cars smaller than anyone had ever seen before, and rode another wave of success. Today, Honda Corporation employed over hundred thousand people in the U.S.A. and Japan. And it's one of the world's largest automobile companies.

Honda succeeded because one man made a truly committed decision, acted upon it and made adjustment on a continuous basis. Failure was simply not considered a possibility. You can do the same thing. What are you planning to do? When you are faced with problems, People will ridicule you, they will mock you, and they will tell you that you cannot do it. But how do you see yourself? Do you see yourself as somebody who will be able to achieve what you have set out to achieve? Or do you see yourself as a failure that they call you? Look at all the names I have mentioned in this book.

Oprah was condemned. She was sacked because her employer said she was not fit to appear on T.V. Oprah was able to change things around to her advantage. Today, we know her to be very successful for her Television programme. Look at Soichiro Honda. He faced so many problems. He committed his time. He sold his properties; he even went ahead to pawn his wife's jewelleries just to achieve what he had set out to achieve. Imagine going out to borrow money to build a factory and it got burnt twice? Not only that. He looked for money again; he built another factory, only to be taken away by earthquake. All these are enough reasons for any man to say he wants to give up. Some people don't even face this much problems before they give up in life. This man refused to give up because he was so sure of himself. He didn't see giving up as an option.

Success story that does not have failure in it is not complete. What makes a true success is what you have been able to learn as a result of past mistakes. How often you were able to rise again when you fall, how you were able to turn the situation around. Successful people work on their past errors. There is a saying that "practice makes perfect". I believe it should be "practice makes better" the more you try something, the better you become at doing it. It will be unreasonable of anyone who is pursuing his dream not to expect to fail. Failure should energise you into doing it better.

Expecting failure is an important step as you pursue your dream. Success stories have problems, chaos, situations, circumstances, obstacles, issues, errors, etc incorporated into it. Without the listed items linked to success, then it is not true success.

Colonel Sanders was 65 years old when he received his first social security cheque of $99. He was broke, and owned a small house and a beat up car.

He made a decision that he has got to change. The only idea he had was a chicken recipe, which his friends liked. With that idea in mind, he took massive action. He left his home in Kentucky and travelled to many states in the US to sell his idea. He told the restaurant owners that he had a chicken recipe that people liked and he was giving it to them for free.

What he wanted in return was for the restaurant owners to pay him a small percentage on the pieces of chicken sold.

He got rejections after rejections, but did not give up. In fact, he got over 1000 rejections.

He got 1009 no's before he got his first yes. With that one success Colonel Hartland Sanders changed the eating habits of the whole world with Kentucky Fried Chicken, popularly known as KFC.
How many of us will keep knocking on doors when we have received 1000 rejections? I presume not many! This is why there are not many successes like Colonel Sanders.

Age is no barrier to success, and so is capital. What is needed is an idea put into action, followed with proper planning and persistency

CHAPTER 5

AVOID DISTRACTIONS

Distraction is the number one drain of your time. It's not the emails, phones, text messages, social media, etc. It's you allowing those things to be a distraction to you in your life. We're generally faced with a barrage of daily distractions and although they usually involve the emails, phones, text messages, and social media referenced above, distractions can also be our friends, family, and/or pets.

Who or what do you allow in to your world to distract you at any time of the day? Once you recognise who or what is the distraction, then you can begin to set up rules and boundaries to control them. Consider scheduling distraction free time. For example, if you're an Internet Marketer... recognising that your mental and physical energy is at its peak in the morning you may want to designate the first two hours of each morning to revenue producing activities. This means phones are turned off and email is inaccessible. Distraction free time should also be created for training, learning new skills, development, etc.

You are not alone when it comes to distractions. It's not easy staying on task when you need to work for hours at a time, but some people are able to do it. The question is: why them and not you? It's funny how all throughout our school days we were never taught how to learn and be focused, even though that's all we did. It was just assumed, and ultimately it was hit or miss on whether or not we ended up knowing how to do those things at all.

Since we're left to our own devices, it's up to us to find ways to master our focus ability.

So without further ado, let's get started.

1. Keep your vision/goals in mind

First things first, why do you even need to focus? Do you want to become a skilled guitar player? Do you want to write a novel? Do you want to start working from home? Think about it. Knowing why we need to stay focused can help us push through the tough and tedious parts of accomplishing our goals. That's when our ability to focus is really tested and when it's most needed.

2. Reduce the chaos of your day by focusing on 2-3 important tasks:

If you have 20 tasks you need done everyday how effective do you think your focus ability will be? Terrible, right? You can't expect to do those things with sophistication if you're too scatterbrained to focus. You need to break it down to the essentials.

Focus on only doing 2-3 important tasks a day (even one is okay), but no more than that. It's all you need to take steps towards accomplishing your goals. Slower is much better than giving up early because you took on too much, too early.

3. Do those tasks as soon as possible

In order to make sure you get those 2-3 tasks done, you need to do them early. This means as soon as you wake up, you're already plotting how to do them. So get up, use the bathroom, eat breakfast, and do it (Yes, BEFORE work is the best time to do it).

It's tough, but waiting to do them only invites distraction to take over. Those distractions will come, and they will drain your willpower. This makes working on your goals harder to do, so don't wait do work on your goals, do them as early as possible.

4. Focus on only the smallest part of your work at a time

An easy way to kill your focus is to see a goal for the big giant accomplishment that it is. Most goals will at least take a few weeks to months to accomplish, and knowing that can make it feel like it'll take forever to do.

This'll cause you to do one of two things:

1. You become discouraged because the goal is too big

2. You fantasize about what it'll feel like to achieve the goal

Either way is terrible for your focus and always a potential problem when focusing on the big picture or using visualisation.

So what should you do? Focus on doing a very small, minimum amount of work instead. For example, what seems easier? The key here is to use minimums, why? Because chances are you'll push past them. Eventually your minimum will increase, and you'll slowly improve your ability to stay focused on the bigger tasks.

5. Visualise yourself working

I briefly mentioned earlier that visualisation techniques can hurt you more than help you sometimes. But there is a proper way of using visualisation, and it's by visualising yourself actually working (not as if you've succeeded already). Champion runners use this technique to great effect, usually by working backwards. They imagine themselves winning at first, then they act out the whole process in reverse, feeling and visualising each step all the way to the beginning. A quicker and more relevant way to apply this would be to imagine yourself doing a small part of the task at hand. For instance, If you need to practice your guitar but it's all the way across the room (let's assume maximum laziness for the sake of this example), what should you do? First, imagine standing up (really, think of the sensation of getting up and then do it). If you really imagined it, visualised and felt the act of standing up, then acting on that feeling will be easy.

Then repeat the visualisation process with each step till you have that guitar in hand and you're playing it. The process of focusing so intently on each step distracts you from how much you don't want to do something, and the visualisations "ready your body" for each step you need done.

All you need to do is apply this process to whatever it is you need to focus on, just start with the smallest motion you need to do.

6. Control your internal distractions: Internal distractions are one of those problems you can't really run away from. You need to find ways to *prepare* your mind for work, and find simple ways to keep it from straying to non-essential thoughts as well. A good way to prime your mind for work is to have a dedicated work station. If you always work in a specific area, then your mind will associate that area with work related thoughts. Simple enough, right? When you take breaks make sure to leave your work station, that way you'll know when you're "allowed" to let your thoughts roam free as well. Deadlines are pretty useful here. This method helps keep your mind from wandering around since you've got that looming deadline coming along. Ultimately though, silencing those unwanted thoughts is all about getting some traction going. So instead of focusing on what's happening internally, focus getting *something* done (anything!). Once you do that, you'll see that all your thoughts will be about finishing your task.

7. Escape from/remove external distractions

This tip is pretty straightforward; just get away from things that distract you. Is the television a distraction? Work in another room. Are the kids distracting you? Get up earlier and work before they wake up. Is the Internet distracting? Turn off the modem. It's usually pretty obvious what you should do, but you still shouldn't overlook this piece of advice.

8. Skip what you don't know

This is a tip I don't see often enough, if you hit a snag in your work then come back to it later. Focus your attention on what you can do, keep working "mindlessly" at all costs. All this means is that you should focus on the easy parts first.

Eventually you can come back to the more difficult parts, and hopefully by then it'll have come to you or you'll have built up enough momentum that it won't break your focus if you work on it.

9. Improve your discipline with focus practice: There are a few focus exercises you can do to improve your overall discipline.

The first one is meditation, which is basically the definition of focus in practice. Think about it, you're literally just sitting there doing nothing. It's a great method for building focus ability, de-stressing, and giving you greater control over your emotions. You should definitely give meditation a shot.

The second exercise is the pomodoro method. These are basically "focus sprints," and each one is followed by a solid break. Like real sprints, you'll get better and better at doing them over time. Each interval improves your ability to stay focused when it matters, so it's more than worth your time to try this out.

10. Manage your momentum

Momentum is like a discipline lubricant—it helps ease the process of sticking with goals. That's why I think it's important that we never take true breaks from our goals; we end up losing momentum and relying on discipline to get back on track (not an easy thing to do).

This means each and every day we need to do something significant to further our goals (yes, even weekends and holidays). And when I say "significant," I don't necessarily mean a big task—but rather, any task that brings us closer to our goals. For instance, if your goal is to be a freelance writer, then write one single pitch on a weekend. If your goal is get healthy, then go for a short 5 minute walk even on Christmas day. Nothing big, nothing crazy, only stuff that is significant enough to contribute to the success of your overall goal.

CHAPTER 6

BE POSITIVE

Life is unpredictable, demanding and full of pressures which certainly play a big role in our ability to look at things from either a positive or negative lens. But…have we ever truly considered the disadvantages of not staying optimistic and positive in all situations, no matter how difficult and challenging?

It is very easy to go down the slippery slope of focusing on the negative and dwelling on the bad things that have happened, and/or the worst case scenarios which only drains us of our energy to be effective, be engaged, be happy and able to get things done. I would like to suggest we take the alternate path and develop the ability to look at the up side of life and maintain a positive attitude even in the worst of times which can make the ultimate difference in leading a happy life as well as a successful career.

Working on your dream requires a high level of positivity and the ability to stay optimistic. We will always experience change which is the only constant thing in life. Our ability to embrace and deal with changes in addition to on-going expectations and demands will require us to maintain a positive attitude and outlook even during adversity. By doing so, we are able to uncover different approaches, tap into unfound potential in ourselves and others, as well as manage stress effectively.

Once upon a time, a man named Paul applied for a new job, but he didn't believe he will get it, since his self-esteem was low, and he considered himself as a failure and unworthy of success.

He had a negative attitude toward himself, and therefore, believed that the other applicants were better and more qualified than him. Paul's mind was occupied with negative thoughts and fears concerning the job, for the whole week preceding the job interview. He actually, anticipated failure.

On the day of the interview, he got up late, and to his horror he discovered that the shirt he planned to wear was dirty, and the other one needed ironing. As it was already too late, he went out wearing a wrinkled shirt and without eating breakfast.

During the interview, he was tense, negative, hungry and worried about his shirt. All this, distracted his mind and made it difficult for him to focus on the interview. His overall behaviour made a bad impression, and consequently, he materialised his fear and did not get the job.

Another man named Daniel applied for the same job too, but approached the matter in a different way. He was sure that he was going to get the job. During the week preceding the interview, he often visualised himself making a good impression and getting the job.

In the evening before the interview, he prepared the clothes he was going to wear, and went to sleep a little earlier. On day of the interview, he woke up earlier than usual, and had ample time to eat breakfast, and then to arrive to the interview before the scheduled time.

Daniel made a good impression and got the job.

What do we learn from these two stories? Was there any magic used? No, everything happened in a natural way. Positive thinking is a way of Life.

With a positive attitude we experience pleasant and happy feelings. This brings brightness to the eyes, more energy, and happiness. Our whole being broadcasts good will, happiness and success. Even our health is affected in a beneficial way. We walk tall, our voice is more powerful, and our body language shows the way we feel.

Positive and negative thinking are contagious. We affect, and are affected by the people we meet, in one way or another. This happens instinctively and on a subconscious level, through words, thoughts and feelings, and through body language.

Is it any wonder that we want to be around positive people, and prefer to avoid negative ones?

People are more disposed to help us, if we are positive, and they dislike and avoid anyone broadcasting negativity.

Negative thoughts, words and attitude, create negative and unhappy feelings, moods and behaviour. When the mind is negative, poisons are released into the blood, which cause more unhappiness and negativity. This is the way to failure, frustration and disappointment.

In order to turn the mind toward the positive, some inner work is required, since attitude and thoughts do not change overnight.

1. Read about this subject, think about its benefits, and persuade yourself to try it. The power of your thoughts is a mighty power that is always shaping your life. This shaping is usually done subconsciously, but it is possible to make the process a conscious one. Even if the idea seems strange, give it a try. You have nothing to lose, but only to gain.

2. Ignore what other people say or think about you, if they discover that you are changing the way you think. The fact that they think you cannot do it does not mean you cannot achieve it. Ignore the negativity of such people and don't let it colour the way you see yourself. Such people are naysayers and should be avoided completely.

3. Use your imagination to visualise only favourable and beneficial situations.

4. Use positive words in your inner dialogues, or when talking with others.

5. Smile a little more, as this helps to think positively.

6. Once a negative thought enters your mind, you have to be aware of it, and endeavour to replace it with a constructive one. If the negative thought returns, replace it again with a positive one. It is as if there are two pictures in front of you, and you have to choose to look at one of them, and disregard the other. Persistence will eventually teach your mind to think positively, and to ignore negative thoughts.

7. In case you experience inner resistance and difficulties when replacing negative thoughts with positive ones, do not give up, but keep looking only at the beneficial, good and happy thoughts in your mind.

8. It doesn't matter what your circumstances are at the present moment. Think positively, expect only favourable results and situations, and circumstances will change accordingly. If you persevere, you will transform the way your mind thinks. It might take some time for the changes to take place, but eventually they will.

9. Another useful technique is the repetition of affirmations. This technique is similar to creative visualisation, and can be used together with it.

Are there any naysayers in your life? Someone who is discouraging you from pursuing your goals and dreams, perhaps? Someone who thinks that you are joking and says "it's impossible!" when you share your grand plans for your future? Someone who sabotages you when you try to cultivate a new habit or quit a bad habit? Someone who is keeping you from achieving your highest potential? Such people are referred to as Naysayers. We all have them around us.

At one point in our life, we are bound to meet naysayers, be it colleagues, acquaintances, friends and family. Naysayers are termed as such because their favourite response is "Nay" say you want to pursue your dream. They will say "Nay" and tell you that it will not work for you and that you will be a failure. They will tell you that what you intend to do will not feasible because of the bad economy. (the economy is always bad to them)

Most of the time, naysayers have little to contribute to the conversation, they only respond to extinguish your hopes and dreams.

When I decided to decided to pursue my dream of becoming a lawyer, a friend told me that i was only going through a phase and I was going to regret it later. Another friend asked me if anyone said i was crazy. Some friends around me advised me not to try it. Each had his/her own set of reasons why it was a bad decision. Some said that economic recession was coming soon and I won't be able to look after my family if i quit my job that was giving me regular income. Some said my job was fantastic and that i would never get such a great job after studying law. Some said that I do not have the skills required and the know-how to achieve success in my new path. Some said that I was wasting my previous education and squashing my career path. I listened to all of them but I followed my dream. I did not let their negativity colour the way I see myself.

Each time I meet a naysayer, I always try to understand where such person is coming from. Does the person have a valid viewpoint, or is he/she just speaking from his/her fears? If it is clear that the person is projecting his/her own fears rather than giving constructive thoughts, I will disregard his/her input. My goals are precious, and I am not going to entertain anyone who tries to dump toxic onto my goals. After i know that someone is a certified naysayer, I will reduce contact with such a person . Because I don't want such a person to project their fears and hang ups into my goals.

Negative people will drain your energy and dim your light. In an attempt to avoid negativity, it is important to deliberately create a positive environment. For example, you can surround yourself with positive people, listen to uplifting music, and/or read inspirational articles and books. When you are seeking to become happier, you must decide that you will seek out positive experiences. What is it that motivates you or makes you smile? The people, places and tasks that you enjoy should consume your downtime. Being alone and bored is a prime opportunity for negative thinking. When you are distracted by having fun, you are less inclined to experience sadness. If you begin to experience negative thinking, write down three positive affirmations that you can immediately say to yourself to counteract your negative thoughts. I also recommend that you practice verbalizing gratitude on a daily basis. Gratitude is a great way to shift your mind and generate positive thoughts. Another great strategy entails differentiating truth from faulty thinking. Ask yourself if you are 100% sure that your thoughts are accurate. Finally, when you are challenged, admit when you are focusing on the problem and not the solution. Focusing on the solution will allow you to shift your energy into problem solving mode. By shifting to problem solving mode, you will be able to focus more on the solution than the problem itself. Negativity perpetuates itself, breeds dissatisfaction and clutters the mind. And when the mind is cluttered with negativity, happiness is much harder to come by.

Here are 10 ways to defend yourself against negativity:

1. **Don't take other people's negativity personally.** Most negative people behave negatively not just to you, but to everyone they interact with. What they say and do is a projection of their own reality – their own attitude. Even when a situation seems personal – even if someone insults you directly – it oftentimes has nothing to do with you. Remember, what others say and do, and the opinions they have, are based entirely on their own self-reflection.

2. **Spend more time with positive people.** You are the average of the people you spend the most time with. In other words, who you spend your time with has a great impact on the person you eventually become. If you are around cynical and negative people all the time, you will become cynical and negative. Does who you are and who you

want to be reflect in the company you keep? Start spending time with nice people who are smart, driven and likeminded. Relationships should help you, not hurt you. Surround yourself with people who reflect the person you want to be. Choose friends who you are proud to know, people you admire, who love and respect you, people who make your day a little brighter simply by being in it.

3. **Be the positivity you want to see in the world.** Lead by example. You can't always save the world, but you can make the world a better place by practicing what you preach – by becoming self-aware, tapping into your compassion, and protecting your positive space. Doing simple things like talking about positive daily events, common friends, hobbies, happy news, make for light conversations with negative people. Keep the conversations focused on optimistic areas the person can relate to. You can disarm their negativity, even if it's just for a little while.

4. **Change the way you think.** The one thing nobody can take away from you is the way you choose to respond to what others say and do. The problem isn't the events that are negative. The problem is the way you react to those events. The last of your freedoms is to choose your attitude in any given circumstance. Complaining, blaming and criticizing aren't going to change the situation. It is not always easy to find happiness in ourselves, but it is always impossible to find it elsewhere. Regardless of the situation you face, your attitude is your choice. Remember, you can't have a positive life with a negative attitude. When negativity controls your thoughts, it limits your behaviour, actions, and opportunities. If you realised how powerful your thoughts were, you would never think another negative thought again.

5. **Focus on solutions.** Negative people have an endless supply of pity party invitations (PPI). Don't RSVP. Oftentimes people use negativity

as a barrier to protect themselves from the world, which in turn blocks them from solutions that could improve their life. Instead, identify solutions. Don't dwell too much on what went wrong. Instead, focus on the next positive step. Spend your energy on moving forward toward a positive resolution. Remember, when you focus on solutions, by thinking and acting positively, sound becomes music, movement becomes dance, a smile becomes laughter, and life becomes a celebration.

6. **Love whoever is around to be loved.** Practice acts of kindness. It's a lot harder to be negative when you're in the presence of love and kindness. Be that presence whenever possible. Let your guard down. Talk to someone you don't know straight from your heart. Compliment them. Don't anticipate awkwardness. Just be you in that beautiful way only you know, and give them the chance to smile and connect with you. Sometimes a kind word and some attention from a friend is all that's needed to turn a negative attitude around.

7. **Provide support when it makes sense.** Some people complain as a way of crying for help. They may not be conscious of it though, so their comments come across as negative complaints rather than requests. Show some concern. Just a simple "Are you okay?" or "Is there anything I can do to help you?" can do wonders. Resist the urge to judge or assume. It's hard to offer compassion when you assume you have them figured out. Let them know they are not alone. People overcome the forces of negative emotions, like anger and hatred, when the counter-forces of love and support are in full effect.

8. **Realise that life is a series of ups and downs.** Acknowledge the negativity, accept it, and let it pass through your consciousness, thereby teaching you a lesson but not ruining your day. Life is full of highs and lows, but you don't have to go up and down with them. We develop from the negatives when we accept them and learn from them. This

cycle is all part of the human experience. Relax, let go a little, and enjoy the ride.

9. **Concentrate on today.** Too often, we carry around things from our past that hurt us – regrets, shame, anger, pain, etc. Holding onto anger is like drinking poison and expecting the other person to die. Don't let these negative points from the past rob your present happiness. You had to live though these things in the past, and although unfortunate, they can't be changed. But if the only place they live today is in your mind, then let go, move on, and be happy. You can decide right now that negative experiences from your past will not predict your future.

10. **Let go and move on when you must.** If all else fails, remove yourself from the wrong situations and relationships. Some people are like dark clouds; when they disappear, it's a brighter day. Know when it's time to let go. Letting go of negative people doesn't mean you hate them, it just means that you care about your own wellbeing. Every time you subtract negative from your life, you make room for more positive.

It isn't easy to remain positive when negativity surrounds you, but remember that you have full control of your attitude. Think of it this way: An entire body of water the size of the Pacific Ocean can't sink a ship unless it gets inside the ship. Similarly, all the negativity in the world can't bring you down unless you allow it to get inside your head. People who are able to discern the positive points in negative situations are the ones who prosper in the long run. So defend yourself against the 'negative way' and make room for a positive day.

CHAPTER 7

PERSISTENCE

Being persistent is easier to say than do, nobody will try to deny that. But it's realising the possible outcome, and being able to see ten miles down the road, that can push you to adopt persistence as a trait of yours. And when someone tells you to be persistent the first thing crossing your mind is rather a mix of qualities that you scarcely ever thought about combined.

Things like immense self-confidence, dedication, discipline, and even stubbornness to an extent are parts of the picture created from the combination that was mixing for a second. And knowing which of those plays its part when the time comes makes quite easier to grasp understanding of what is to be persistent.

I've heard this listening to a great legend in the self-improvement and personal growth industry, Sir Les Brown.

He has said so many empowering things, that it's hard to track even a tiny percentage of his quotes, inspirational sayings and so on. But this one was a story, analogy if you will, that changed my perception when it comes to being persistent.

So here it goes:

I don't know whether you've heard about this Chinese Bamboo tree. It's a tree quite nothing like any other. After being planted it takes about five years to start growing above the ground.

But all that time whilst you are wondering if it will make it, and assuming that those five years pass you will not see the results, it requires constant care. You must water it each and every day, fertilize the soil, and create the right conditions in order for it to grow.

Now here is the thing — once it starts to grow above the soil, ***it grows 90 feet tall in six weeks.*** *You heard right,* ***90. And in six weeks.***

So there was a man according to Mr. Brown's story who planted a Chinese bamboo tree in his garden. And every day he watered the soil, fertilized it from time to time, and in a way nurtured the tree. This went on for a long time, since the tree needed five years to pass in order to break ground.

Around that time all folks from the neighbourhood started to make fun of him and ridicule him for watering couple of inches of ground every day. People crossed by his house and often times said things like: "Hey, what are you doing? The rumour around the neighbourhood goes that you are growing a Chinese bamboo tree. That's right?"

The man recognising the scepticism refused to make that his reality, and only answered: "Yes". And often times there were jokes on his expense where people pointed out that there is nothing there, but bare soil.

But this man was what I truly envision as persistent, and as time went by he was more determined and knew that each day passing, he was closer to his goal. And after five years passed, something wonderful happened – **the tree finally peaked through the ground, and in couple of weeks it went higher than everyone could have imagined.**

All of the neighbours now watched, and started to change their behaviour. They went to him, and tried to convince him that they believed in the whole thing from the beginning. "I told you that you were going to make it now, didn't I" they said.

And that's the thing you see, once you move closer to success, not only that every bit of your scepticism dies, but people around you that never took what you are doing seriously, all of the sudden believe in you a great deal now.

Had this man at any point stopped watering and nurturing the tree, it would have died right in the ground.

But that's the thing about being persistent- you invest in whatever that is that you do without seeing instant results; sometimes you don't see results for a very long time, just as in this story, but you keep your phase any way. Have patience and engage in consistent action – that's what Mr. Less says. The results will come; it's a matter of time.

I will like to share a story with you; If you are familiar with success book, titled, "Think and grow rich", you might remember the story in that book about a man who gave up his quest for gold too soon during the California gold rush long ago. The story goes like this: From months upon months this man went about prospecting for gold in hills. Somehow he just knew that he will strike gold. Every day he got up early and walked to the hills in search of his fortune. He dug and dug with his simple tool, he found gold here and there but never anything to write home about. The story goes that he finally gave up digging because he could not find the mother gold he was searching for.

Hearing this, another prospector came to him and offer to buy all the tools he's got. The man agreed and sold his tools for whatever money he would get for them. This prospector then went on to hire a land surveyor and engineers and geologist and they all combined their knowledge and went to work on the land which the first man had been digging before without result. It was told that upon studying the area and the mine, the men discovered that the first man had been literally three feet from where he would have reached the gold he wanted.

Literally three feet! This poor prospector who had given up was so close to the gold, he could reach and touch it but there was no way he could know this because he gave up too soon and did not take the proper tools for this job. Picture that! Imagine somebody who woke up in the morning and decided he was going to go after something. He tried for weeks; weeks ran into month and month into months when he was about to get that which he had longed for, he gave up.

The major difference between those who could not make it and those who made it, is the fact that, those who made it refused to give up and just like this man who gave up, those who could not make it, quit trying. This man would have been able to achieve what he had set out to achieve. He only laboured in vain because all that which he did, somebody came and benefited from it. It is good to be persistent.

How to be persistent

If you ask me for a secret formula, there isn't any. It's rather more of an understanding of when you should keep pushing, and on what to count when the time comes.

- *First of all you must be stubborn as the guy in the story.* Go against everybody if you feel that it's the right thing to do.

- *Being persistent is sometimes no more than having discipline.* If you make yourself disciplined enough and hold on to whatever routine that you put together, it's just a matter of time as I said. Having discipline in a way helps you go through those moments when your stubbornness takes a hit.

- *In order for you to be persistent you must first be determined.* Know what you would like the outcome to look like. Envision it on daily basis, picture yourself reaching it, enjoying the fruits of your work and persistence.

- *Believe in your goal, all the time, every time.* Because if you don't, it's less than likely that you will invest yourself and keep going when things like doubt in yourself, or doubt in your goal take place. If you find it difficult sometimes (as many of us do), just empower yourself by listening to some motivational speakers, have a conversation with a friend that supports you, read some inspirational quotes, or just strengthen your determination and faith in yourself whatever way you find suiting for you.

Do not let other people's opinion become your reality.

Being persistent, you are being taken more seriously not only in the eyes of others, but also in front of your own eyes. Once you put faith in yourself, it's not long before others start to see that, and also give you more credit. Being persistent, you succeed eventually, and then start to inspire people and by your actions convince them to have a go on their dreams too.

Here's the most important point here: Find a compelling reason to succeed that is more than just the money and you energize your mind for success. Make yourself to have a reason so great for succeeding, that there will be no other option but being persistent.

No matter what you do in life, there will be times when things don't go according to plan, times when everything seems to be working against you and times when you fail. At moments like these, you feel like giving up, and may even suffer from a reduced sense of confidence and self-esteem that makes you feel bad about yourself. The easy thing to do during such times is to quit what we are doing and move on to something else. Something that's easier or distracts us from our previous task. This is exactly what the large majority of people in our society do, because it is natural human tendency to do the things that are fun and easy over those that are hard and necessary. Unfortunately, this often leads to long-term failure in life, because those who quit whenever they experience failures or problems will never stick with something of real significance long enough to truly benefit from it. But those who are able to keep going through periods of adversity stand a much better chance of achieving something of real meaning and value in life.

If you want to achieve real success in life, you must be willing to stick with something for the long-term and avoid the tendency to view things from a short-term perspective.

Most people who fail in life, for example, expect to become successful quickly and with minimal effort. Whilst, this may happen for some people, the majority of us will have to work very hard before we accomplish what we set out to achieve. This is the true reality of success. "Persistence"

Only a small minority of people , however, will be willing to do this long enough for them to achieve their goals. Those who are successful, persist. Those who are not, don't.

One of the most important lessons that i have learnt in life is that no matter how bad something seems, there is invariably something positive that can be taken from a negative experience. There have been many times in my life, for example, when something happened to me that was uncomfortable or painful to deal with, but looking back on that event months or even years later, I realised that it made me a stronger and better person.

Of course, no one likes to experience difficulties or misfortunes in their life, but the fact is that these things will happen to you at some point or another. You can therefore either choose to give up when the going gets tough , or persist until you achieve your aims and objectives in life. Very often you will find that if you persist through difficult times, you will learn something that helps you to progress even further than you could before.

As a result, I now view failures in my life not as failures, but as valuable learning experiences that I can use to better and improve myself with.

Another interesting thing that I have observed is that my greatest successes have often come after my greatest failures. It's almost like there is some kind of mystical force in the universe that is testing me to see how much I really want something. Even though it may seem hopeless at the time, eventually, by working long enough, I have almost always been able to complete what I set out to do.

If you can adopt this mentality of trying to see the good in every situation, you will find it a lot easier to develop the skill of self persistence. You will also find that when things don't go your way, you will be able to cope much better with it emotionally.

This is important as one of the biggest destroyers of persistence are feelings of self-doubt and depression. These negative emotions can zap your motivation, essentially draining you of the energy that you require to do something

So the next time that a bad event happens to you, take some time to think about how you could possibly benefit from it. Ask yourself, what lesson can I learn from this experience? How is this going to make me a better person? You may not always be able to come up with an answer immediately because if a particular experience has resulted in a stronger emotional reaction such as anger, sadness or despair, the emotions that you are feeling will interfere with your ability to think logically and rationally. But given enough time, you will eventually be able to find some good from a situation no matter how bad what happened to you was.

Persistence is a very important trait to develop in life because it is ultimately interlinked with one's own personal development and self – improvement. You will only get better in life by failing at things, learning from those experiences and moving on.

In order to do this, however, you must also have the persistence or determination to keep on going and not to give up. Without persistence, your ability to grow and develop as a person will be severely restricted, and so will be the amount of success, wealth and happiness that you will be able to achieve.

The experiences we have in life ultimately shape the type of person that we become. As a result, sometimes you will find that what you thought you wanted in the past isn't what you want right now.

HOW TO BE A MORE PERSISTENT PERSON

- **Think long term**
  Recognise that things of value will probably take you a lot of time and effort to achieve. If you hope to get rich quick or become an overnight success, you will quickly become discouraged when things get difficult and so will probably give up easily if you don't get the quick result you have anticipated.

- **Set goals**
  Having goals focuses your mind on what you want to achieve. Get into the habit of goal setting and set yourself both short and long term goals to break down your main goal into series of smaller and more manageable chunks. Remember, there is no one step that does it, it's a lot of little steps that will do it. When you complete a goal, give yourself a reward for its completion as this will help to further motivate you to achieve future goals.

- **Learn and be positive**
  You can learn from anything that happens to you in life, regardless of whether it was a good or bad thing that happened to you. Use what

you learn to improve yourself so that you become a stronger, more experienced and wiser person.

- **Read books**

  One way to motivate yourself through periods of difficulty is to read books about people who have gone through difficult times in their life but eventually became successful at what they were doing. This might involve reading biographies of people who you admire.

- **Pay the price**

  This means that if you really want something in life, you will have to make some sacrifices in order to get it. Usually, this will involve choosing how you manage your time, such as whether you want to spend your time watching TV or working on your business instead.

- **Visualise what you want**

  Mentally imagine or picture the thing you want to achieve. Think about how good it would be to have or accomplish it, the way it would make you feel and the benefit you will gain from it. Do this before you fall asleep at night and you will help to programme that image into your subconscious mind, which will then motivate you to keep on working towards the realisation of your dream or ambition during the day.

- **Watch your negative emotions**

  Negative emotions cause you to respond to things using the emotional or middle part of your brain. This region of the brain tends to result in irrational thinking which subsequently leads to poor decision-making. If you find yourself becoming overly emotional about something, do not make any important decisions in this frame of mindset because the decision which you make will likely not be the correct or best decision.

- **Adapt to change**

  Even though you may have a clearly laid out plan for the accomplishment of your aims and objectives, very rarely will you find that you are able to follow your plan exactly.

  Things will change and be different from how you expected them to be, and so you need to be flexible enough to adapt to this change if you are to see your plan through to completion.

Note

Note